WEEKLY WR READER
EARLY LEARNING LIBRARY

Great Americans

Benjamin Franklin

Monica L. Rausch

Reading consultant: Susan Nations, M.Ed., author/literacy coach/
consultant in literacy development

Please visit our web site at: www.garethstevens.com
For a free color catalog describing Weekly Reader® Early Learning Library's list of high-quality books, call 1-877-445-5824 (USA) or 1-800-387-3178 (Canada). Weekly Reader® Early Learning Library's fax: (414) 336-0164.

Library of Congress Cataloging-in-Publication Data

Rausch, Monica.
Benjamin Franklin / by Monica L. Rausch.
p. cm. — (Great Americans)
Includes bibliographical references and index.
ISBN-13: 978-0-8368-7682-6 (lib. bdg.)
ISBN-13: 978-0-8368-7689-5 (softcover)
1. Franklin, Benjamin, 1706-1790—Juvenile literature. 2. Statesmen—United States—Biography—Juvenile literature. 3. Scientists—United States—Biography—Juvenile literature.
4. Inventors—United States—Biography—Juvenile literature.
5. Printers—United States—Biography—Juvenile literature.
I. Title.
E302.6.F8R195 2007
973.3092—dc22
[B] 2006032579

This edition first published in 2007 by
Weekly Reader® Early Learning Library
A Member of the WRC Media Family of Companies
330 West Olive Street, Suite 100
Milwaukee, WI 53212 USA

Managing editor: Valerie J. Weber
Art direction: Tammy West
Cover design and page layout: Charlie Dahl
Picture research: Sabrina Crewe
Production: Jessica Yanke and Robert Kraus

Picture credits: Cover, title page, pp. 6, 7, 10, 15, 17, 18 © The Granger Collection, New York; pp. 5, 9, 12, 14 © North Wind Picture Archives; p. 8 Charlie Dahl/© Weekly Reader Early Learning Library; p. 13 © Robert Holmes/CORBIS; p. 19 Library of Congress; p. 20 U.S. National Archives and Records Administration; p. 21 Courtesy of the Franklin Institute, Philadelphia, PA

Printed in the United States of America

1 2 3 4 5 6 7 8 9 10 10 09 08 07 06

Table of Contents

Cover and title page: Benjamin Franklin worked to free the American people from British rulers. He was also an author, scientist, and inventor.

Chapter 1

A Young Ben Franklin

On a Sunday morning in 1723, Deborah Read looked out of her doorway into Philadelphia's streets and saw an odd young man walking along. He was taking a bite out of a large bread roll, and he carried two more under each arm. His pockets were stuffed with socks and other clothing, and he looked dirty.

© North Wind Picture Archives

Read did not know it, but she was looking at her future husband, Benjamin Franklin. Franklin had just arrived in the city with only enough money to buy bread. Franklin, however, had great skills in reading, writing, and printing, and he was a hard worker. He would become a famous writer, printer, **statesman**, **inventor**, and thinker.

Later that day in Philadelphia, Franklin gave two of his bread rolls to a woman and her child.

Benjamin Franklin was born on January 17, 1706, in Boston, Massachusetts. He was the tenth son of his father, Josiah Franklin. Benjamin had a total of sixteen brothers and sisters!

Franklin's father wanted him to learn a trade. When he was twelve years old, Franklin began learning the printing business from his older brother, James.

THE [Nº 80

New-England Courant.

From MONDAY February 4. to MONDAY February 11. 1723.

The late Publisher of this Paper, finding so many Inconveniencies would arise by his carrying the Manuscripts and publick News to be supervis'd by the Secretary, as to render his carrying it on unprofitable, has intirely dropt the Undertaking. The present Publisher having receiv'd the following Piece, desires the Readers to accept of it as a Preface to what they may hereafter meet with in this Paper.

Non ego mordaci distrinxi Carmine quenquam,
Nulla venenato Litera onista Joco est.

LONG has the Press groaned in bringing forth an hateful, but numerous Brood of Party Pamphlets, malicious Scribbles, and Billingsgate Ribaldry. The Rancour and bitterness it has unhappily infused into Mens minds, and to what a Degree it has sowred and leaven'd the Tempers of Persons formerly esteemed some of the most sweet and affable, is too well known here, to need any further Proof or Representation of the Matter.

No generous and impartial Person then can blame the present Undertaking, which is designed purely for the Diversion and Merriment of the Reader. Pieces of Pleasancy and Mirth have a secret Charm in them to allay the Heats and Tumors of our Spirits, and to make a Man forget his restless Resentments. They have a strange Power to tune the harsh Disorders of the Soul, and reduce us to a serene and placid State of Mind.

The main Design of this Weekly Paper will be to entertain the Town with the most comical and diverting Incidents of Humane Life, which in so large a Place as *Boston*, will not fail of a universal Exemplification: Nor shall we be wanting to fill up these Papers with a grateful Interspersion of more serious Morals, which may be drawn from the most ludicrous and odd Parts of Life.

As for the Author, that is the next Question. But tho' we profess our selves ready to oblige the ingenious and courteous Reader with most Sorts of Intelligence, yet here we beg a Reserve. Nor will it be of any Manner of Advantage either to them or to the Writers, that their Names should be published; and therefore in this Matter we desire the Favour of you to suffer us to hold our Tongues: Which tho' at this Time of Day it may sound like a very uncommon Request, yet it proceeds from the very Hearts of your Humble Servants.

By this Time the Reader perceives that more than one are engaged in the present Undertaking. Yet is there one Person, an Inhabitant of this Town of *Boston*, whom we honour as a Doctor in the Chair, or a perpetual Dictator.

The Society had design'd to present the Publick with his Effigies, but that the Limner, to whom he was presented for a Draught of his Countenance, descryed (and this he is ready to offer upon Oath) Nineteen Features in his Face, more than ever he beheld in any Humane Visage before; which so raised the Price of his Picture, that our Master himself forbid the Extravagance of coming up to it. And then besides, the Limner objected a Schism in his Face, which splits it from his Forehead in a strait Line down to his Chin, in such sort, that Mr. Painter protests it is a double Face, and he'll have *Four Pounds* for the Pourtraiture. However, tho' this double Face has spoilt us of a pretty Picture, yet we all rejoiced to see old *Janus* in our Company.

There is no Man in *Boston* better qualified than old *Janus* for a *Couranteer*, or if you please, an *Observator*, being a Man of such remarkable *Opticks*, as to look two ways at once.

As for his Morals, he is a chearly Christian, as the Country Phrase expresses it. A Man of good Temper, courteous Deportment, sound Judgment; a mortal Hater of Nonsense, Foppery, Formality, and endless Ceremony.

As for his Club, they aim at no greater Happiness or Honour, than the Publick be made to know, that it is the utmost of their Ambition to attend upon and do all imaginable good Offices to good Old *Janus* the Couranteer, who is and always will be the Readers humble Servant.

P. S. Gentle Readers, we design never to let a Paper pass without a Latin Motto if we can possibly pick one up, which carries a Charm in it to the Vulgar, and the learned admire the pleasure of Construing. We should have obliged the World with a Greek scrap or two, but the Printer has no Types, and therefore we intreat the candid Reader not to impute the defect to our Ignorance, for our Doctor can say all the *Greek* Letters by heart.

~~*His Majesty's Speech to the Parliament,*~~ October *11. tho' already publish'd, may perhaps be new to many of our Country Readers; we shall therefore insert it in this Day's Paper.*

His MAJESTY's most Gracious SPEECH to both Houses of Parliament, on Thursday *October* 11. 1722.

My Lords and Gentlemen,

I Am sorry to find my self obliged, at the Opening of this Parliament, to acquaint you, That a dangerous Conspiracy has been for some time formed, and is still carrying on against my Person and Government, in Favour of a Popish Pretender.

The Discoveries I have made here, the Informations I have received from my Ministers abroad, and the Intelligences I have had from the Powers in Alliance with me, and indeed from most parts of Europe, have given me most ample and current Proofs of this wicked Design.

The Conspirators have, by their Emissaries, made the strongest Instances for Assistance from Foreign Powers, but were disappointed in their Expectations: However, confiding in their Numbers, and not discouraged by their former ill Success, they resolved once more, upon their own strength, to attempt the subversion of my Government.

To this End they provided considerable Sums of Money, engaged great Numbers of Officers from abroad, secured large Quantities of Arms and Ammunition, and thought themselves in such Readiness, that had not the Conspiracy been timely discovered, we should, without doubt, before now have seen the whole Nation, and particularly the City of *London*, involved in Blood and Confusion.

The Care I have taken has, by the Blessing of God, hitherto prevented the Execution of their trayterous Projects. The Troops have been incamped all this Summer; six Regiments (though very necessary for the Security of that Kingdom) have been brought over from *Ireland*; The States General have given me assurances that they would keep a considerable

James printed a newspaper called the *New-England Courant*.

Franklin loved to read the newspapers and books James printed. When he was sixteen years old, Franklin wanted to write for James's newspaper. His brother, however, thought he was too young. Franklin decided to write letters to the newspaper. He signed the letters "Silence Dogood." James and his friends thought the letters were funny and smart, and James printed them.

James read the letters Franklin wrote. He did not know that Franklin was "Silence Dogood."

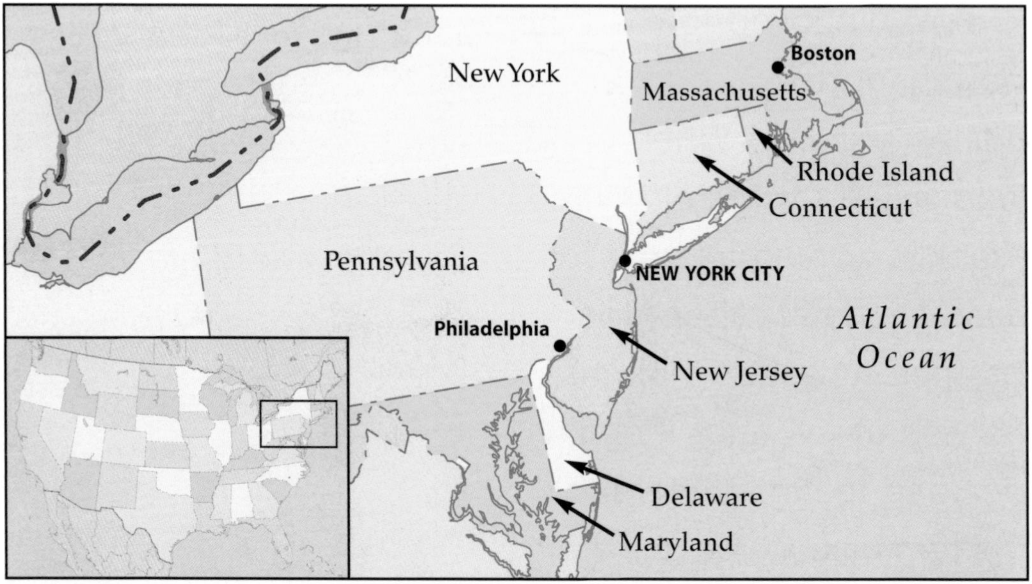

Franklin traveled by boat from Boston to New York. Then he walked through part of New Jersey before reaching Philadelphia by rowboat.

Franklin finally told James that he wrote the letters. James's friends could hardly believe the teenage boy could write so well! James, however, was angry. Soon, he and Franklin began to fight. Franklin decided to run away to Philadelphia.

When Franklin reached Philadelphia, he found a printing job. He also stayed with the Read family and became friends with the Reads' daughter, Deborah.

Franklin worked very hard as a printer, but he wanted his own printing business. The governor of Pennsylvania noticed how hard Franklin worked. He promised to give Franklin money for printing equipment if he went to England to buy it.

The governor of Pennsylvania, Sir William Keith (in green) wanted to help Franklin.

Deborah Read was happy to see Franklin when he returned to Philadelphia. He did not look like the boy she once saw carrying rolls of bread!

In 1724, Franklin set sail for England. While traveling, he found out that the governor had broken his promise. Franklin had no money for the printing equipment or to return home! He was not afraid, however. When he arrived in England, he quickly worked to earn money.

In 1726, Franklin finally returned to Philadelphia. There, he married Deborah Read. Together they would raise two sons and a daughter.

Chapter 2

The Printer and Writer

Two years after Franklin returned, he found a business partner. He finally opened his own printing business. Franklin began printing a newspaper. It soon became the most popular paper in the American **colonies**.

Franklin also wrote a yearly almanac called *Poor Richard's Almanack.* The almanac had weather reports and other information. Franklin included his own sayings, such as "A penny saved is a penny earned."

Poor Richard's Almanack became the best-selling book in the colonies. It sold over ten thousand copies a year!

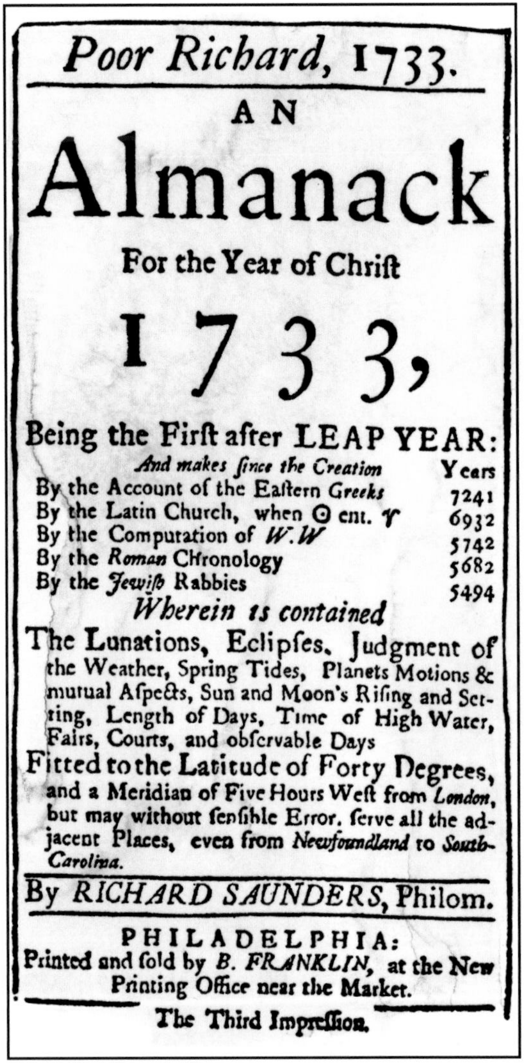

Poor Richard, 1733.

AN

Almanack

For the Year of Chriſt

1733,

Being the Firſt after LEAP YEAR:

And makes ſince the Creation Years

By the Account of the Eaſtern *Greeks*	7241
By the Latin Church, when ☉ ent. ♈	6932
By the Computation of *W. W*	5742
By the *Roman* Chronology	5682
By the *Jewiſh* Rabbies	5494

Wherein is contained

The Lunations, Eclipſes, Judgment of the Weather, Spring Tides, Planets Motions & mutual Aſpects, Sun and Moon's Riſing and Setting, Length of Days, Time of High Water, Fairs, Courts, and obſervable Days

Fitted to the Latitude of Forty Degrees, and a Meridian of Five Hours Weſt from *London*, but may without ſenſible Error, ſerve all the adjacent Places, even from *Newfoundland* to *South-Carolina*.

By *RICHARD SAUNDERS*, Philom.

PHILADELPHIA:
Printed and ſold by *B. FRANKLIN*, at the New Printing Office near the Market.

The Third Impreſſion.

During the 1730s and 1740s, Franklin worked to make life better for the people of Philadelphia. He organized a volunteer fire department and found ways to pave and light the streets. He also organized a public library, so everyone could have books to read for free.

Franklin also helped start the Pennsylvania Hospital in Philadelphia in 1751. It is the oldest hospital in the United States.

In 1748, Franklin quit the printing business. He was only forty-two years old, but he wanted to spend time studying science and helping the government. Franklin had already invented some useful items, including the Franklin stove and swimming flippers.

The Franklin stove did not use as much wood as a fireplace and put out more heat.

Franklin also did many experiments with electricity. At the time, people did not know exactly what lightning was. Franklin proved that it was electricity. His writings on electricity were printed in England and in France. He soon became known as a great scientist.

Franklin wanted to see if lightning was really electricity. He flew a kite during a thunderstorm. Franklin had to be careful. A bolt of lightning could hurt or kill him.

Chapter 3

A Great Statesman

In 1757, the people of Pennsylvania asked for Franklin's help. They were unhappy with the Penn family who governed Pennsylvania. They sent Franklin to the king of Great Britain to discuss their problems. The king ruled all the American colonies, including Pennsylvania.

Franklin returned from Britain in 1762, but he was soon sent back. Just after Franklin arrived in England, the British Parliament passed a law that taxed the colonies. The people of the colonies thought the law was unfair. They were angry!

Franklin asked the British Parliament to get rid of the law. Finally, Franklin realized the British did not care about what people in the colonies thought. He knew it was time for the colonies to be independent.

Franklin tried to tell the British that the people of the colonies were angry. The British did not listen.

Franklin returned to the United States in 1775, just one month after the first shot of the **American Revolution** was fired. He met with leaders from the other colonies to talk about the colonies' independence.

On July 4, 1776, the colonies' leaders approved the Declaration of Independence. Franklin was one of the men who signed it.

The American leaders knew Franklin was popular in France. They also knew they needed France's help to win the war. They sent Franklin to France to speak with the French king. In 1778, Franklin finally convinced the king to help the Americans.

Franklin met King Louis of France and signed an agreement with him. The king would send ships to help the Americans fight the British.

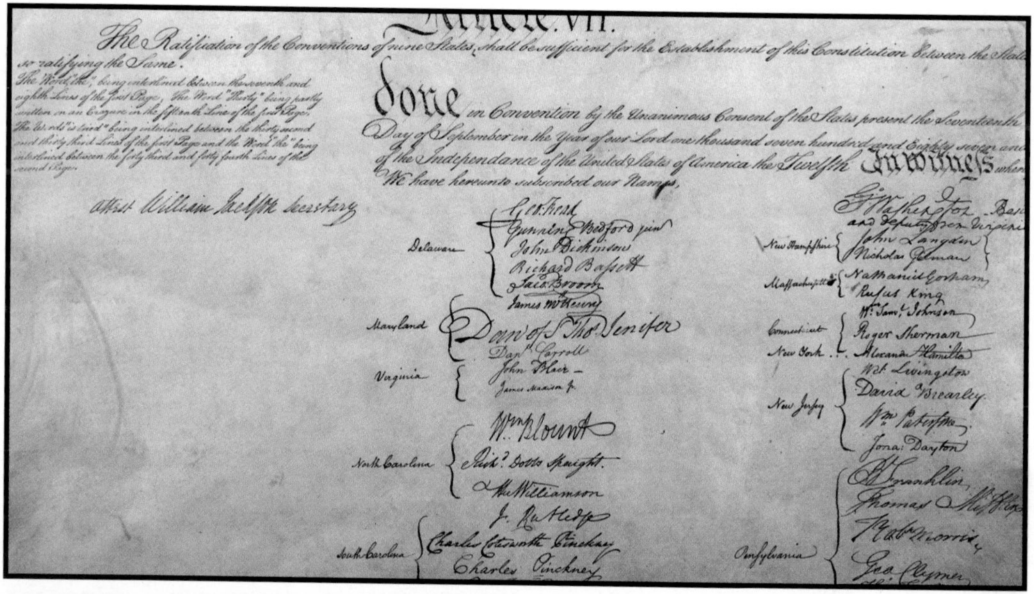

The Ratification of the Conventions of nine States, shall be sufficient for the Establishment of this Constitution between the States so ratifying the Same.

done in Convention by the Unanimous Consent of the States present the Seventeenth Day of September in the Year of our Lord one thousand seven hundred and Eighty seven and of the Independance of the United States of America the Twelfth In witness whereof We have hereunto subscribed our Names,

Attest William Jackson Secretary

Go: Washington Presidt and deputy from Virginia

Delaware: Geo: Read, Gunning Bedford jun, John Dickinson, Richard Bassett, Jaco: Broom

Maryland: James McHenry, Dan of St Thos Jenifer, Danl Carroll

Virginia: John Blair, James Madison Jr.

North Carolina: Wm Blount, Richd Dobbs Spaight, Hu Williamson

South Carolina: J. Rutledge, Charles Cotesworth Pinckney, Charles Pinckney

New Hampshire: John Langdon, Nicholas Gilman

Massachusetts: Nathaniel Gorham, Rufus King

Connecticut: Wm Saml Johnson, Roger Sherman

New York: Alexander Hamilton

New Jersey: Wil: Livingston, David Brearley, Wm Paterson, Jona: Dayton

Pensylvania: B Franklin, Thomas Mifflin, Robt Morris, Geo. Clymer

In 1787, Franklin met with colony leaders to sign the U.S. Constitution. The Constitution was a plan for the new nation's government.

With the help of France's ships, the Americans won the Battle of Yorktown – and the American Revolution. The colonies were free! Franklin finally came home in 1785. He was greeted as a hero who helped win the war.

Franklin died on April 17, 1789. He had come to Philadelphia as a boy with just pennies in his pocket. When he died, people knew him as a great statesman, writer, and thinker. Now, the city of Philadelphia has many landmarks named for this amazing and hard-working man.

The Franklin Institute in Philadelphia honors Benjamin Franklin's work in the sciences. The institute also has many objects that Franklin once owned.

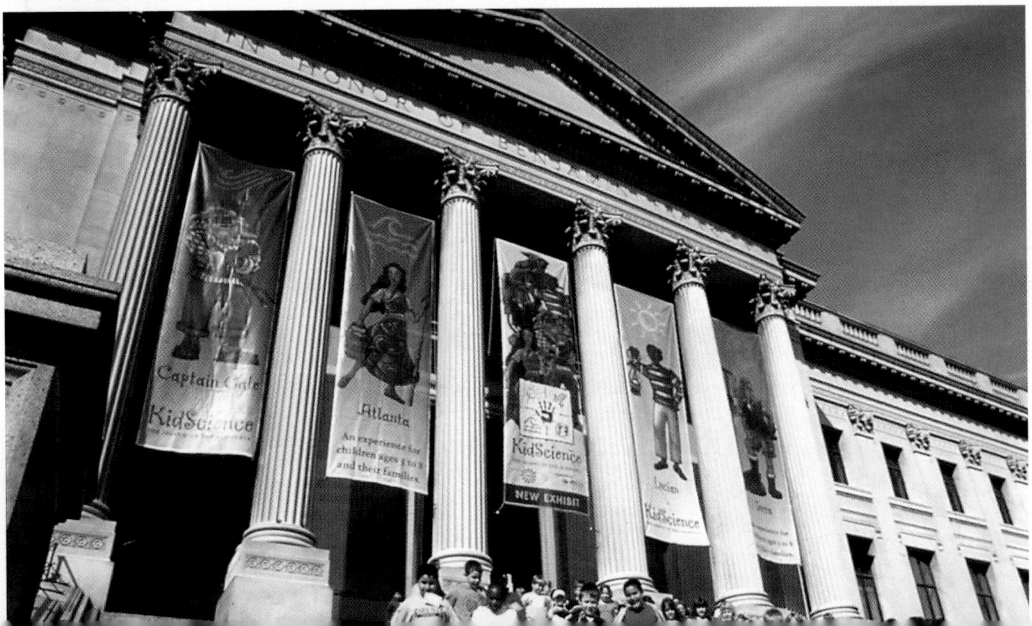

Glossary

almanac — a book containing a variety of facts and other information, such as information on the weather, often organized by the times of the year

American Revolution — the war fought between Great Britain and its American colonies for the colonies' independence

colonies — lands and people ruled by another country

Declaration of Independence — the statement made by the American colonies telling Great Britain that the colonies were free

inventor — someone who creates or designs an object for the first time

landmarks — important buildings or artworks

Parliament — the part of the British and some other governments that makes laws

statesman — a respected government leader or worker

taxed — charged a fee by the government to pay for the government's services

trade — the skilled practice of a specific job

volunteer — describing work done without pay

For More Information

Books

Now and Ben: The Modern Inventions of Benjamin Franklin. Gene Barretta (Henry Holt and Company)

Benjamin Franklin. Lives and Times (series). Jennifer Blizin Gillis (Heinemann)

Benjamin Franklin. Real People (series). Philip Abraham (Scholastic Library)

Web Sites

Hero History: Benjamin Franklin
www.imahero.com/herohistory/ben_herohistory.htm
Information on the life of Benjamin Franklin

Time for Kids: Benjamin Franklin
www.timeforkids.com/TFK/specials/articles/0,6709,1076243,00.html
Information and quizzes about Benjamin Franklin

Publisher's note to educators and parents: Our editors have carefully reviewed these Web sites to ensure that they are suitable for children. Many Web sites change frequently, however, and we cannot guarantee that a site's future contents will continue to meet our high standards of quality and educational value. Be advised that children should be closely supervised whenever they access the Internet.

Index

About the Author

Monica L. Rausch has a master's degree in creative writing from the University of Wisconsin-Milwaukee, where she is currently teaching composition, literature, and creative writing. She likes to write fiction, but sticking to the facts is fun, too. Monica lives in Milwaukee near her six nieces and nephews, to whom she loves to read books.